To Tim
Best wishes
Sam

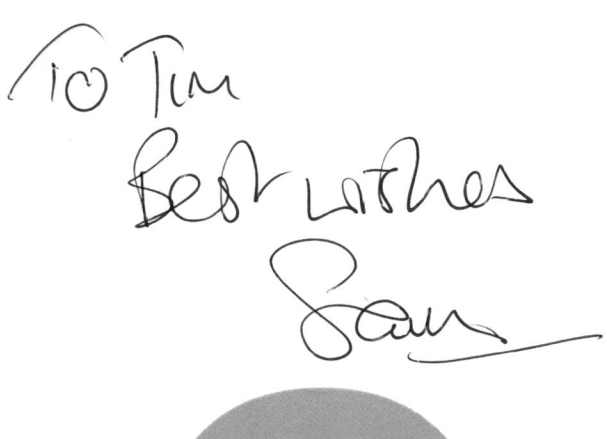

habits

for a happy and productive day

by Harley Street performance coach

SAM DYER

Printed in the United Kingdom.
First printed July 2019.
First edition.

Publisher: Independent Publishing Network
Publication date: July 2019
ISBN: 978-1-78972-437-0 (Paperback)
Author: Sam Dyer
Email: hello@samdyer.co.uk
Address:
Kemp House, 152-160 City Road, London, EC1V 2NX
Website: samdyer.co.uk
Please direct all enquiries to the author.

*This book is dedicated to
my wife, Cara, my children
and everybody who has helped to
shape me both personally
and professionally
over the years.
Truly, thank you.*

Contents

Habit 9 - Meditation

Daily routine

Foundations

Sam Dyer

About the author

I was born in Oxford, England in 1976. I have four daughters and yes, that certainly does keep me busy!

Professionally, my background is in sales and marketing. I started off during college days working in the telesales department at Olan Mills, a photographic portrait studio. That was great fun and I learnt a lot. Most weeks, I topped out my commission and cleared the raffle out because I got the most referrals.

I have worked for very small companies right up to Yell Group (home of Yellow Pages) being the largest and most corporate. The range in size of companies has given me insight and experience at every turn. I take something positive from everything and everyone.

In 2009, I was made redundant after five years as one of the UK's largest business brokerages. I started a marketing company, which I thoroughly enjoyed... most of the time.

I became interested in Neuro Linguistic Programming (NLP) after meeting someone called Chris Menlove-Platt, an NLP trainer, through networking. From 2013, that journey took me through a one day introduction course, my NLP Coaching Practitioner course, which was spread over 12 months and then my NLP Master Practitioner course, which was spread over another 12 months.

During the Master Practitioner course, I realised that I wanted to make my business life one that involved training and coaching on a full time basis. Thankfully, I had some very understanding co-directors at the marketing company, who allowed me to make that transition. I started by doing coaching and training alongside and then gradually increased it whilst decreasing the marketing.

My business is centred in London and I have a consulting room in the world-famous Harley Street, an achievement I am very proud of. Even from an early age, I have had an aspiration to be in Harley Street. It has only been now where I have actually been in a profession which has allowed me to.

Coaching and training gives me great job satisfaction and it is a continuous journey of learning.

This year saw the addition of completing my firewalk instructor training. Now, I offer rebar bending, block chopping, arrow snapping, trust falls, glasswalks and, of course, firewalks as part of empowerment days.

Empowering other people is the best feeling ever and fits with my purpose of helping people lead a life more powerful.

As we fast approach the mid-point of 2019, I am very excited about the events and collaborations being discussed for opportunities within the UK, Europe, Malaysia and Africa.

Introduction

Why is it that in so many areas of our life, we understand the need to prepare and yet when it comes to work we often just go straight into it?

If you undertake any type of physical exercise, you will know the importance of warming up (and cooling down). Sports people spend time getting themselves in the right frame of mind. So do actors, so do singers and many more.

Everyday millions of people go to work with no plan in place, no time spent on preparation and certainly no time whatsoever spent on getting into the right mindset. For many, the day starts with checking email through blurred vision on a phone which has spent the night next to the bed. That is even worse than not being prepared for the day: it is inviting the outside world in to run your day for you. I know this because I used to do it too!

How many times have you got to the end of the working day and could not really explain what you had actually done? Or maybe you have said things like "I didn't get to do a single thing I wanted to today"?

As Jim Rohn, a well-known entrepreneur and author said: "either you run the day or the day runs you".

This book is about offering a different and better way to run your day. It has made a massive difference to me and I truly want to share it with you.

HABIT 1: exercise

Habit 1 - Exercise

Start small and make it a value

If this is a new habit, start small. For me, physical exercise was never a priority. Whilst I recognised it as a resourceful behaviour, health as a value was so low down the list, it never got a look in. Recently, I did some work around my values and have recognised health and therefore exercise as being part of my 'work' value. This is much higher for me, so I have been able to prioritise exercise.

Our values are something that we live our life by - a set of moral codes you could say. Some are contextual, ie they apply to work or home or being a parent etc. Some are core values, which remain fixed in any context. They are normally expressed as one or two words, often linguistically known as a nominalisation (where a verb has been made into a noun). So, you will recognise values yourself, such as: happiness, health, honesty and so on.

I do a lot of coaching and have found clients find understanding their values very helpful, both in terms of their personal values and creating them for businesses. A 'values elicitation' is the technique used to find out what the values are and then place them in a hierarchy.

Understanding the hierarchy is important. In a

personal set, it allows us to understand why we prioritise different activities or why we respond in a certain way to situations.

In a business context, it is great to bond people together, communicate to the outside world what you stand for as well as speeding up decision making.

Each of us has a belief around what a value means. A belief will typically be described in one or two sentences.

I have facilitated this following exercise many a time and it is something you can do with other people:

Take a value such as 'integrity'. It is a great one to use as most people will hold it as a value.

Ask each to describe what it means to them. If you have five people in the room, you will definitely get five different (yet similar) answers. There are no right or wrong answers as each of us has every right to believe what it means to us from our own map of the world.

Sometimes, we have values which conflict with one another. Sometimes, we have values that we would like to change the position of in the hierarchy. Coaching will definitely help that and there are some very specific NLP techniques which will do just that.

So, understanding your values may well help you, as it did me. By starting small, it makes it manageable too. Do not try to run a marathon on week one! What is the first smallest step you can take?

Do something every day

Yes, every day! Even if it is just a walk around the block. The aim of the game is to get away from your desk or screen; to get some fresh air; to get your blood pumping. On that basis, it really does not have to be anything formal. Playing with your kids, walking your dog, even walking to the pub for lunch counts in my opinion.

Remember, I am approaching this from the point of view of creating the right mindset for the day. If you have certain fitness goals, you may need a different routine.

I like to go to bootcamp three mornings a week and do two workouts at home. That is my Monday to Friday routine. It is not always possible to get to bootcamp, if I am away travelling, for example. In those instances, I will do a home workout version in the hotel room or work with resistance bands or do yoga. On the weekend, I will simply make sure that I do something that is at least a little energetic, such as walk into town with my family. It is only a ten minute walk and yet it is up a big hill.

By doing something every day, you are far more likely to turn it into a habit - more of that later.

Something you like
I think this is crucial. If you absolutely hate running, do not take up running. I know it may sound obvious and yet it is not. It is too easy to get caught up in what other people suggest or what you read about or perhaps what falls in line with your understanding and beliefs.

For example, if you are someone who wants to manage their weight down - which is a positive way of stating "lose weight" - you may believe that cardiovascular exercise is the best way to go. If you like CV, then that is great. If you do not, it is best to find something else that you do like.

Here are just a few examples of things you could do:

Cycling
Walking or running
Gym classes or circuits
Personal trainer sessions
Swimming
Dog walking

Mix it up
If you are going to make exercise a daily habit, you will need to be flexible about what you do. If, like me, you are frequently away for work, be

prepared to alter your routine accordingly.

You will also need to consider how much time you have available each day and the environment around you. If you want to go surfing seven days a week, does it fit in if you have to drive two hours to get to the nearest beach? That is assuming there is sufficient surf too!

In the same way, if you take up weight training, what can you do on days where you do not have access to equipment?

If you mix what you do, remain flexible and take your environment into consideration. There is no reason why you cannot do something every day.

Movement gets blood pumping and feeds the brain with oxygen. It also realises natural endorphins, so it makes you feel good.

As Tony Robbins says: motion makes emotion!

How do you get your energy?
Do you get your energy from inside yourself or from other people? It may well be something that you have never thought about before.

There are various behavioural preference tests, such as Myers-Briggs Type Indicator (MBTI), which come from the Jungian school of psychology. You can even take a free one at 16personalities.com

In terms of how you get your energy, imagine a line with extraversion at one end and introversion at the other. It is not binary, it is a continuum. So, if you are three quarters of the way towards extraversion, you could say you are 75% extraversion. It is contextual to an extent and yet less so than other behavioural preferences.

As a quick insight: if you are the type of person who thrives on being around others and comes away from a social situation feeling very awake, then you get your energy from others, therefore being higher up on the extraversion end. If you find you often put headphones on to drown out noise, like to go off for lunch on your own in a quiet spot and find social situations tiring, then you are higher up on the introversion end of the scale.

So, why is this relevant for exercise? I register at somewhere like 90% extraversion in the context of exercise. That means that I very much get my energy from being around other people. When I am at bootcamp with 20 other people, it really keeps me going. I find a solitary workout much harder because I have less energy due to being on my own, hence often opting for yoga when not at bootcamp.

Externally referenced vs internally referenced
How do you know when you have done a good job? Write down a description of what you think

or get someone else to ask you and record your answers for you.

If you are someone who tends to says things like "if the boss/client is happy, I am", or seeks feedback, you are externally referenced.

If you have a feeling inside or 'just know' that you have done a good job, then you are internally referenced.

I am externally referenced and like to get feedback. This is another reason why bootcamp works well for me. I get feedback from Matt Luxton, our instructor, throughout the session. So, if my form needs adjusting, I know immediately.

Shouts of encouragement from other team members are often heard, especially when we are really pushing ourselves. That all works for me.

If you are externally referenced, consider taking up something where you get feedback from an instructor, a partner or other team members. If you are internally referenced, you may prefer something solitary.

Turn into habit
21 days or 28 days to make/break a habit has been a common belief for a long time. University College London (UCL) carried out research in 2009 where findings showed individual results

as anywhere from 18 to 254 days to form a new habit or cease an existing habit, with the average being 66 days.

What is says to me is that we are all different and that the length of time it takes will depend on a range of factors, such as:

- how strongly you feel about it
- what length of time you have been doing the unresourceful behaviour for
- your support network
- whether you have chosen the right new behaviour for you
- if you have the right environment

I am sure there could be many other factors too.

Top tip:

Rather than aiming for a number of days by when you consider the habit to have been successfully created, think of it as simply being the way you now lead your life.

Action plan

....

....

....

....

....

....

....

....

....

....

....

....

....

Don't forget to include by when you will complete each task by.

HABIT 2: know your why

Habit 2 - Know your why

Find your true purpose

If you find your true purpose, it will keep you motivated and on-track to identify and achieve your goals. As the old quote goes "Love what you do and you will never have to work a day in your life". My understanding is that this quote is often attributed to Confucius and yet the source is actually unknown.

Whoever did say it has a very good point though. If you are loving what you do to generate an income, it will be enjoyable and fun, so therefore not feel 'work-like'.

If you have a sense of purpose which you consciously understand and are able to concisely communicate, you will find that you are able to bring your life into alignment with your purpose much more readily.

In my book (which this actually is, ha!) I think there is nothing worse than leading a life of mediocrity. How many people do you know who are going through the motions each day? If all you are doing is clock-watching at work, going home and putting the television on, then repeating it on a daily basis, do you feel like you are really living life to the full? Is that you right now?

I do a lot of coaching and in my experience, a lot

of people are far closer to knowing their purpose than they either realise or are ready to realise.

Almost all of the time, what holds people back is either fear or lack of confidence or both. Zig Ziglar and Tolly Burkan both talked about FEAR as being False Evidence Appearing Real. Think about it.

We fear loss. We fear rejection. We fear failure. All of these are based on future scenarios. Now, I know you could argue that you need to be realistic and I do get that. For example, I know I do not have a strong enough voice to be a rockstar, nor would I want the life that goes with it. I do love music and performing though. One of the presuppositions of NLP is that if it is possible in the world, it is possible for me. The only question is how specifically. I also know that being a rockstar is not my true purpose.

Can I bring elements of being a rockstar into my work though? I certainly can. Being in front of an audience certainly feels like being a rockstar to me, especially when there is music involved.

My purpose is to help people lead a life more powerful. I embrace that for all that it means and it took destroying a huge limiting belief I had for over 20 years for me to be able to fully step into that purpose.

Everyone has a purpose. Everyone.

Lose the fear and increase the confidence. Confidence is a state and so it is a case of learning how to create that state and apply it in the context you are in. Everyone has confidence, even if it is only confidence that they have no confidence! That is something that can definitley be worked on.

Law of Attraction
The Law of Attraction is all about attracting that which we focus on. So, it stands to reason that if we focus on our purpose, that which comes into our lives will align with achieving that purpose. If Law of Attraction is not something you particularly believe in, I am sure that you will agree that when we act with purpose, we are more open to and aware of opportunities which help us achieve.

Call it Law of Attraction, being focused, sending out the right vibes, being on the right wavelength or in tune with the universe - I do not mind what works for you. The important part is that you know your purpose and start acting with that in mind.

Who do you know that has drama in their life on a daily basis? Who do you know that goes through life with everything going their way?

Do you expect the best or do you expect the worst? Human nature is dictates that we like to prove ourselves right - it is called 'confirmation bias'. Think of a day where you stubbed your toe getting out of bed and then it all went downhill from there. It can be very easy to let ourselves slide like that. It takes more effort to stop yourself from spiralling and get the day back on track. It is 100% worth the effort!

Have you ever bought a new car? It does not matter whether it was brand new or used. Do you remember suddenly being aware of that exact same make and model car everywhere you went? When you bought the car, you were ultra-aware of that make and model, possibly even the age and colour too.

The reason I bring it up at this point is to link it in with the LOA (Law of Attraction). If you are open to opportunties around your purpose, you will start to see them around you and recognise them.

1)   Know your purpose
2)   Be alive to opportunity
3)   Take action

Your Reticular Activating System (RAS) is a network of neurons in your brain stem. It filters in information deemed relevant and filters out information deemed irrelevant. So, you could say that this literally is what creates your own reality. It is your unconscious which informs your RAS what to filter in.

If you believe that life is full of difficulty and scarcity then that will be your experience of it.

If you believe life to be full of abundance and opportunity, then that will be what you experience.

Our brains do not understand the difference between a visualisation of something we wish to be and something that already is. That is why daily visualisation is so important. You must also really believe it. See what you see, hear what you hear, feel what you feel. If you can, also add a smell and taste to it! The more senses involved, the better.

Spend time on big questions

We are very good at keeping busy. In fact, it is something which is largely applauded in Western society. Often, starting early and finishing late at work is an accolade, the Litmus test to show you are putting it all in.

I often hear people asking others if they are busy by way of small talk, which has an effect of over-popularising its use and reinforces the belief that being busy is always a great place to be.

Being busy fills time. When we fill our time up, we are operating in the here and now. Sometimes, we do this by being present and at a high level of conscious awareness. At other times, we are running on auto-pilot, barely taking notice of our actions.

Whilst 'being present' is important, it is not always where we need to be. Do you ever give yourself time to think? I mean really think. Perhaps a whole morning on your own, unplugged, alone. How about a day?

By not giving ourselves time to think, we ignore life's big questions:

• why am I here?
• what is my purpose?
• what brings meaning to my life?
• what can I do for the greater good?
• how can I truly serve?

There are, of course, many more big questions.

Take some time for yourself. Often, we need to slow down in order to speed up.

Nanodecisions
According to some reports, we make up to 30,000 decisions every day. Once you have removed sleep, that is nearly 2,000 an hour. A lot of those decisions will be made unconsciously - that is to say, those that we are not consciously aware of.

Without getting into the contentious area of what constitutes a decision, what this does make me realise is that we make a lot of decisions every single day.

I think, on the whole, we are good at recognising the times and topics in our lives which we perceive as 'big decisions'. Take, for example, who we marry, the houses we buy, changing jobs and so on.

Where it is often easier to make decisions which are not in our best interest is on a daily basis.

We are highly governed by our emotions or our state. This is also affected by our physiology.

How do we make great nanodecisions? By keeping the following areas in a good place:

1) Sleep
2) Diet
3) Hydration
4) Routine
5) Emotional, physical, spritual, mental wellbeing

If you are in a good place with the above, you are far more likely to make that one more sales call, try that little bit harder, smile more often and all make all those other nanodecisions in the best way possible for you.

What can you do?
Every one of us is unique. We have a unique experience of life. Each one of us is the sum of

everything that has gone before us. Think of those moments that hold significance in your life; the people who stand out; the experiences which you would say have shaped you.

Aside from that which you are very aware of, there are so many more experiences, people and moments which have made an impact on you. It is one of the reasons why each one of us is unique.

On top of that, each of us has our own subjective reality in any case. So, even if two people were to live two entirely identical lives, each would have their own perspective - their own reality.

Use your uniqueness to your advantage.

How can you best use everything you know?

What are you better placed to do than anyone else in the world?

What does not feel like work?
Remember: "Love what you do and you will never have to work a day in your life"?

It is so easy to make the assumption that we cannot earn a living from doing what we love doing. Often, that is a limiting belief. Are there other people out there making a living from your favourite hobby? If it is possible for them, it is possible for you too - the only question is how specifically.

If you love surfing or dealing with people or making things, can you make a living from doing just that? Have you ever tried? What would happen if you did?

Keep it in mind daily
Out of sight, out of mind. Once you have perfectly crafted the wording or image which represents your 'why', keep it somewhere that you can see it.

It is helpful to place it somewhere so that it can serve as a regular reminder of why you are doing what you are doing, especially when the going gets a little tougher.

Let it inform everything else
Being aware of and remembering your purpose can inform various choices that you make. For example, if your purpose is to be the best personal trainer in your area, then drinking and eating too much every weekend is unlikely to be in alignment.

Quote:

As Mahatma Gandhi famously said:

"Be the change you wish to see"

Action plan

....

....

....

....

....

....

....

....

....

....

....

....

....

Don't forget to include by when you will complete each task by.

Habit 3 - Goals

Set your goals, otherwise where are you going?
Alice: "Would you tell me, please, which way I ought to go from here?" Cheshire Cat: "That depends a good deal on where you want to get to." Alice: "I don't much care where –"
Cheshire Cat: "Then it doesn't matter which way you go."

Do not be like Alice! And, do not let your business be like Alice either.

Goal setting is so important. If you do not have specific goals, how do you know if you are heading in the right direction? Yes, wanting to be successful, for example, is great... and yet, how do you know when you have achieved it? What will you see, hear, feel?

I frequently meet people who are like Alice and often they do not realise it.

Spend half a day or a day on thinking about what you want to do and how you are going to get there. I think drawing it can often help and yet that will depend on your own preference - do whatever suits you best. You may wish to get a coach involved if you need some help.

Context is key

Make sure you are aware of the context of your goals. Are they business related? Are they in relation to your family? Are they specific, such as buying a new house? Make sure you keep the context the same throughout your goal setting exercise. It is great to create separate sets of goals. Make sure you check if there are any conflicts.

Use PACER

I think PACER is an excellent model for goal setting and is superior to SMART(ER) and GROW.

There are variations on the theme of SMART and SMARTER. I would suggest that the version on the left is the more commonly-known.

Specific	Specific
Measurable	Meaningful
Action-orientated	Agreed
Realistic	Relevant
Time-bound	Time-bound
Evaluate	Ethical
Readjust	Recorded

GROW stands for:
Goal - Reality - Options - Way forward

Whilst these all have their merits, personally I find PACER to be better for goal setting. In particular, PACER pays attention to the ecology of what is surrounding you. For example, if you want to study for an MBA and already have four children and two businesses, can you commit the time? PACER also covers resources needed, which could include money, knowledge, time, equipment and more.

Utlimately, use whatever works for you. I would definitely advocate using some sort of framework for goal setting.

P is for Positively stated
Make sure it is stated in the positive – that means stated as something that you will work towards rather than something you should avoid. Losing something or stopping something are likely to lead to avoidance strategies, as we do not like loss, so ask the question of yourself "What do I want instead?".

A is for Achievement
What are your measures of achievement that will tell you that you have succeeded? What will you see, hear and feel that provides you with that sensory-based evidence that tell you that you have got it?

C is for Context
This is the opportunity to define with whom, where and when you want this outcome and also with whom, where and when you do not want it? Is there a specific length of time that this is valid?

E is for Ecology

This is about considering the effect of your achievement upon the wider system of your life (either professional, personal or as a whole). Who else will be affected and how will they feel (includes clients, customers, family, line managers) and what might the effect be upon the whole organisation? What might you have to give up in order to achieve this outcome?

R is for Resources

Consider everything that you might need to support you in achieving this outcome. As well as material things such as equipment, IT or finances, there may be other people that you could role model as they have already achieved this before you. In addition, you need to recognise what you need within yourself including the qualities and skills that you already have or may need in the future.

Postively stated
Achievement
Context
Ecology
Resources

How do you eat an elephant?

Like me, there have probably been times in your life where you have put off starting something simply because of not knowing where to begin. If the task or goal seems too large to tackle, it can stop us in our tracks.

How do you eat an elephant? One bite at a time! I am not suggesting you actually eat an elephant of course - the point is that you should break do your goal into bite sized chunks. If you have a huge task ahead of you, what is the single smallest step you could take to start? When are you going to do that? Answer those two questions and you have already committed.

As with many things in life, getting started is often the hardest part - so make a start, however small it is.

The more you procrastinate, the harder it becomes to actually gain traction. What is the first smallest step you can take today?

When I was writing this book, I found it hard to get started. There was so much I wanted to tell you and to get across. I started by first mapping out the names of the chapters, then sub-headings of what each chapter would contain, then getting a few paragraphs down for each sub-heading. If I had not managed to break it down, it would still be some kind of half-formed idea in my head.

Year plan

A yearly plan should be big picture. Look at the overarching themes that you wish to concentrate on and the big goals for the year. 'Write a book' is the kind of level that you should be at with a year plan.

6 week plan

Quarterly plans are too long for my liking. I think that during a three month period, we tend to lose momentum and it becomes too easy to spread things out.

A six week period allows an overarching focus in a particular area. It can be anything which suits you: gain new clients; a new website; staff development.

Week plan

The week plan can be completed at the start of the week, outlined at the start of the week or even done on a daily basis. I like to outline the week before starting, so often this is a Friday, Saturday or Sunday activity.

I use sprints for my working day (see Habit 4).

Remember:

If you do not set goals, how do you know where you are going?

Do not be like Alice!

Action plan

....

....

....

....

....

....

....

....

....

....

....

....

....

Don't forget to include by when you will complete each task by.

BIT4: Sprints

Habit 4 - Sprints

Cannot constantly sprint

A sprint, by its nature, is short. Take sport as an example: the strategy for running 100m is different to that for a marathon. And yet, when it comes to life, particularly business, why do we think we can do the 100m pace all of the time?

To effectively make best use of time, is it important to plan, get in the right mindset, work and take regular breaks.

If you think you are constantly sprinting, you are kidding yourself.

Productivity vs hours

There are at least two generations still in the workforce who have been brought up with the belief that the more you work, the more you get. Time is money. Hard work pays off.

I started my research into this area by actively looking for ways to increase the hours that I could work, such was my mindset at the time. I had heard that you could stay awake by taking a 30 minute nap every four hours, provided that you kept precisely to the timing.

It did not take me long to find that there is substantial research, proving that there is a direct correlation of a drop in productivity in relation to the length of time worked. So, in fact, it would support the exact opposite to the paradigm of "the more you work, the more you get".

Simply working less time, for most, will not be enough. It is important to examine what is being done during a day and how to maximise time. After all, we all have the same 1,440 minutes each day - it is how we choose to use them.

I looked at a number of examples of working patterns and found two which particularly appealed to me for being easy to implement in a wide variety of businesses.

Pomodoro technique
Developed by Francesco Cirillo in the late 1980s, it takes its name from the Italian word for tomato, as he used a tomato-shaped timer whilst at university. There are also suggestions that it comes from the tomatoes which have four sections visible if you cut the top off.

It works as follows:

25 minutes work, then 5 minutes break
25 minutes work, then 5 minutes break
25 minutes work, then 5 minutes break
25 minutes work, then 5 minutes break
15-20 minute break

Cirillo worked in IT, where this has the added benefit of taking people away from their screens, something which I feel is hugely important. I have a client who has a cafe/brasserie. They implemented a version of this technique to move people around different stations, such as the till, coffee machine, milkshake station etc. It can also be used to create variety.

Draugiem Group

This Latvian brand creation company reversed engineered what their top performers were doing. What would you expect this to be? In early? Gone late? At the desk all day?

Remember phrases like "lunch is for wimps"?

They found that the top 10% of users of their DeskTime productivity tracking software worked for less than eight hours a day and took regular breaks.

Typically, patterns were around 52 minutes of work, followed by a 17 minute break. Do you find that surprising? I know I did at first. It seemed to me that 52 minutes of work followed by 17 minutes break is a lot of break.

Unlike the Pomodoro technique, this came from what was already happening. Pomodoro, to me, offers a very focused way of working and the five minute breaks provide little more than a time off-screen and for fluids in and out.

Draugiem's findings imply a rythym. It is a pattern of working and breaking that is not beholden to what the clock says, so can we deduce that it is more 'natural'?

My own take
I think it is very important to try techniques out and find what works best for you. It is also true to say that some job roles are more attendance-based than productivity-based and yet could effectiveness be increased by better working practices?

I found that the 'Draugiem technique' as I dubbed it, was difficult to implement due to the strange ratio. I tried 50 minutes of work with 15 minutes break and again found it difficult to plan. So, I went for 50 minutes on and 10 minutes off, making a nice and easy to manage hour block, which I call a sprint. I normally start my sprints on the hour or half hour, depending on what fits in best with the day.

Taking a regular break definitely keeps me more alert. I expected that anyway. What I did not expect was the increase urgency I found I created in myself. I always plan the day in advance and I frequently find myself thinking that I must get a task done within one sprint, whereas before it may have dragged on for longer. If you have ever lived in a house bigger than you needed, you will have no doubt managed to fill it up. We do exactly the same with time if we do not place some boundaries on ourselves.

The flipside is that I am also better at not over-filling my day with unrealistic expectations of what can be completed.

Some days, I may choose to only have four sprints of work due to family commitments. By deciding this in advance, along with what I want to get covered, the pressure of unrealistic expectations are alleviated and I can focus more readily and clearly.

Flexibility
It is important to keep a degree of flexibility in what you do. Afterall, I cannot realistically expect travel time, meeting durations or coaching sessions to fall neatly within my allotted sprints.

Holistic productivity
Another eureka moment for me was the realisation that being a peak performer requires success in all areas of life. We are very good at dressing domestic work up as leisure time. Spending Saturday morning washing the car, cutting the grass, cleaning the house - it is still work!

I am a big fan of homeworking, at least for part of the week, if not all. When you work from home, you can do things like put the washing on or take half an hour before starting another sprint to clean the bathroom. Suddenly, productivity as a whole increases.

Remember:

Production decreases over time worked

Take regular breaks

Action plan

....

....

....

....

....

....

....

....

....

....

....

....

....

Don't forget to include by when you will complete each task by.

HABIT 5: create your own change

Habit 5 - Create your own change

The technique
(Looking down)
Talk to yourself and ask yourself "What do I want to do differently?". Then say to yourself "If I could do that, what would it look like?". As you say this, lead your eyes to looking up.

(Looking up - seeing yourself within the image)
Be dissociated from the image. In other words, watch yourself doing the new behaviour. Notice what happens to your state and the effect upon other people involved.

(Step forward)
Associate with the whole experience by stepping into it physically and metaphorically. Become yourself doing the new behaviour.

(Allow your eyes to track down again)
This is important as it allows you to evaluate your new behaviour in terms of you and your values.

Ask yourself "What adjustments do I have to make so that this sits more comfortably?".

If you need to make any adjustments, lead your eyes to back up and do so.

Re-run the process at least 3 times (even if you are maintaining the new behaviour).

Future Pace
It is important for you to check how the behaviour feels in circumstances that you might encounter in the future. In NLP coaching terms, this is known as "Future Pacing".

Think of a situation in which the new behaviour is part of your response to it. Picture yourself in that situation and be associated and in yourself. Deploy the new behaviour and monitor what is happening around you and how you are feeling. Are you feeling comfortable or is there some feeling of disquiet or discomfort inside you? If so, this normally means that you are contravening your own values.

Ask yourself "What changes do I need to make this to align with my values so that I feel congruent and one with myself?".

Re-run the cycle again in this new situation with the changes or adjustments.

The other vital part of the NBG is to tap into the feelings you feel when in your desired state...

... see what you see
... hear what you hear
... feel what you feel
... taste what you taste
... smell what you smell

The greater the number of senses and depth of sensory experience you can place on it, the better. Taste and smell are very strong senses, so what will achieving your goal taste and smell like?

How to self-coach

The New Behaviour Generator technique is an excellent example of how you can coach yourself. Other ways to coach yourself include asking yourself the right question.

If you are thinking of doing something, ask yourself what would happen if you did not.

If you are thinking of not doing something, ask yourself what would happen if you did.

Other great questions to ask around goal-setting are:

If I achieve this goal, what will I get?
If I achieve this goal, what will I not get?
If I do not achieve this goal, what will I get?
If I do not achieve this goal, what will I not get?

These are simple yet highly effective tools to self-coach and ascertain what the right thing to do is.

Self-coaching can be done at pretty much any time. Give yourself the time and room to think. Often a run or a drive helps because it occupies your conscious mind, which in turn helps open up and access your unconscious mind.

Top tip:

When you do the New Behaviour Generator, load as many senses on to your future state as you can.

Believe it!

Action plan

....

....

....

....

....

....

....

....

....

....

....

....

....

....

Don't forget to include by when you will complete each task by.

HABIT 6: motivation

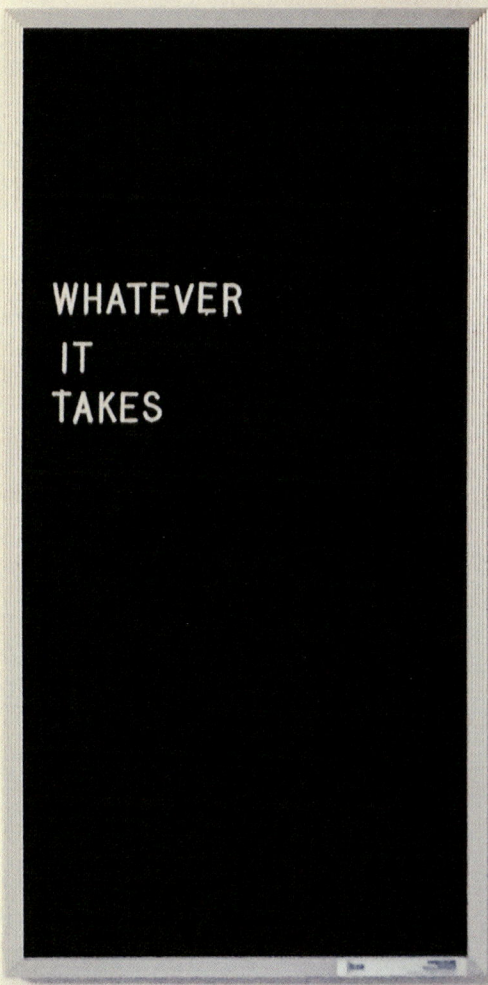

Habit 6 - Motivation

Visualisation board

Our brains are fantastically powerful. Neuroscience has shown that congnitively, we cannot tell the difference between something that we imagine and something that is real. I think this makes good logical sense as we can only ever construct our own subjective version of reality in any case.

Creating a visualisaion board works well to keep motivation levels up and also remind us of why we are doing what we are doing, even when times are tough.

"Out of sight, out of mind" is very true in this context, so make sure your board is somewhere you can easily see. You may like to create a visualisation board screensaver.

Fill the board with all of those things that you are striving for which motivate you. It could include:

Family
Clock to represent time
Holiday destinations
Dream house(s)
Dream car(s)
Private school
Trust fund image

Whatever is right for you, is right!

Draw your future
To do this exercise, I like to use a large sheet of paper, say from a flip chart pad. Alternatively, you can tape or staple A4 together up to the size you wish.

Draw a representation of where you are right now in life. If you are not quite where you want to be, include a shouty boss, broken down car or whatever it might be.

On the same face of the paper, draw where you want your life to be. Take a context of within a year or five years or however long suits you.

Now look at the difference between the two.

What do you need to do to make it happen?
How will you turn your dream into reality?
What is the first smallest step you can take today?

Watch videos
There are a huge range of motivational videos freely available on the internet. Find what works best for you and get a variety which you can catalogue with links and a short description. Some days, you may want something that is intellectually stimulating. Other days, you may need a good kick to get you going.

TEDtalks are another fantastic source of knowledge and motivation. It is a free platform which you can access directly through their website, app or even from a smart tv now.

Quotes
I am a huge fan of motivational quotes. They can be very powerful: sparking thought, creating and maintaining motivation, bringing light to darkness.

I am also very aware that there are a great many quotes out there on the internet, especially in the form of memes, which are misquoted, misguided or complete nonsense. So, before liking or sharing (or believing!) take some time to consider what is says. If it is attributed to someone, carry out some basic due dilligence to see if it is authentic.

Here are three of my absolute favourites:

Mahata Gandhi
"The difference between what we do and what we are capable of doing would suffice to solve most of the world's problems"

Henry Ford
"Whether you think you can or you think you cannot... you are right!"

Marianne Williamson

"Our deepest fear is not that we are inadequate. Our deepest fear is that we are powerful beyond measure. It is our light, not our darkness that most frightens us. We ask ourselves, Who am I to be brilliant, gorgeous, talented, fabulous? Actually, who are you not to be?"

Pre-plan week's worth of motivational material
It does take some time to search through, look at, watch, check authenticity etc. As you start to build up your own catalogue of quotes, videos, images, soundbites and whatever else you think is useful, it becomes far easier to plan ahead.

I think it works best to pre-plan your week of viewing, otherwise it can really distract from what you are trying to achieve.

Towards/away
According to the LAB Profiling work of Shelle Rose Charvet, approximately 40% of us are mainly 'towards' people and around 40% are mainly 'away from' people. The remaining 20% are a mixture of both.

Get someone to help you on this by recording your answers. Take each one of your goals and ask the following questions. I will take an example of 'gain £20k of new revenue'.

Q: What is your goal?
A: To get £20k of new revenue.

Q: What is important to you about getting £20k of new revenue?
A: It will give me more stabliity and a good financial buffer.

Q: Why is that important to you?
A: I will be able to concentrate and focus more with knowing that money is in the bank.

The above illustrates how someone who is mainly 'towards'. Note how the language is towards a goal and how the motivation behind goes towards something too.

Q: What is your goal?
A: To get £20k of new revenue.

Q: What is important to you about getting £20k of new revenue?
A: I do not want to be unstable and have no financial buffer.

Q: Why is that important to you?
A: I will not be able to concentrate and will not have enough focus if I do not know that I have enough in the bank.

The above illustrates someone who is mainly 'away from'. Note how the language centres on things they do not want, ie things that they wish to get away from. In goal setting, you may remember that goals are always to be stated positively, that is to say 'towards' language. By doing this, we ensure that we know what the goal is and will therefore be able to ascertain when it has been achieved, with the correct parameters in place.

Find out your motivation for each of your goals. Regardless of your preference, you may find some goals are towards, some are away from and some are a mixture of both.

Whatever works for you!
Perhaps most importantly: whatever works for you is the right thing!

Education
For any of us to grow, we need to expand our knowledge. I am not talking about doing a university degree and yet if that is right for you, do not let me stop you.

I only read non-fiction books and get a great deal from them. Audio books are great too. I normally read one or two books a month and watch over five hours of motivational/educational videos per week. This is made up of TEDtalks, YouTube videos and even some things on Netflix.

It is great to look for parallels and lessons in daily life too. Very often I will hear something or experience something which then makes me think of something else which teaches me a lesson. If something goes wrong, what can you learn from it? If you learn something from it then it ceases to be a problem and becomes something positive instead.

Be bold enough to go off your beaten track too. I am proud to say that my network includes a huge array of diverse people and by mixing with them I learn new things. As an example, until a few weeks ago, I did not even know that a 'gong bath' existed. I have met shaman, yogis and even an exorcist - all of whom open my mind in different ways.

Welcome challenging your assumptions and beliefs. You will learn, grow and ultimately become a better person.

Quote

Henry Ford

"Whether you think you can or you think you cannot, you are right"

Action plan

....

....

....

....

....

....

....

....

....

....

....

....

....

Don't forget to include by when you will complete each task by.

HABIT 7: plan

Habit 7 - Plan

We all have the same amount of time available each day. What we choose to do with that time, the state we are in and the attitude we have, is what makes the difference.

As Jim Rohn famously said "either you run the day or the day runs you". The habit of planning is important and effective. What are you going to do with your 1,440 minutes each day?

In my experience, many people use urgent and important as interchangeable terms. They definitely are not and each has a distinct meaning.

Important is something of value, of impact. Urgent means that it is time-sensitive.

I find Stephen Covey's Time Management Matrix very helpful.

Covey's quadrants
In Covey's matrix, there are four quadrants:

1   urgent, important
2   not urgent, important
3   urgent, not important
4   not urgent, not important

Where do you spend most of your time? Where do you think you *should* spend most of your time? His view was that the best situation is to be spending most of your time in quadrant 2 and some in quadrant 1. By adopting this, you are likely to show: vision, perspective, discipline, control. You will also have few crises.

	Urgent	**Not Urgent**
Important	Crises Pressing problems Deadline-driven projects	Prevention Relationship building New opportunities Planning Recreation
Not Important	Interruptions Some calls Some mail Some reports Some meetings Pressing matters Popular activities	Trivia Busy work Some mail Some phone calls Time wasters Pleasant activities

The idea is that you take time from quadrants 3 and 4. By spending more time in quadrant 2, you will in turn reduce the amount of time needed in quadrant 1 due to the prevention measures you will be putting in place.

Start by considering what you have been doing over the past few days. In which quadrant(s) have you most been spending your time?

Something you may have to do even more of is saying "no" to people so that you can increase your focus and time on the things you know that you should be.

In line with weekly/quarterly planner

It is very easy to fill our time with activity which seems worthwhile and yet does not actually contribute to meeting our goals. When you are planning out your days, check that the activity aligns with your goals and your quarterly planner. If it does not and yet you still feel it is important to do, question if it is the right time. If yes, you may need to adjust your goal and/or planner. If not, schedule if for another time or possibly cross it off your list entirely.

Keep to time

It is important to keep to time. If you are utilising my sprint method, please do not be tempted to start 'flexing' the time as the day goes on. Of course, if you are in the middle of an important call, do not hang up. I know from experience that if you go over time on the first sprint and possibly the second, it becomes very difficult to stick to the regime. What you definitely do need to keep is some flexibility over content and yet make sure that you are not actually being sidetracked.

Be realistic

In the past, I know I have been unrealistic with how long I have allowed for certain tasks or how much I expected to complete in one day. For your planning to be effective, make sure that you are realistic with what you can get done and how long you need to spend on things.

Time for thought

Allow yourself time to think. Often, you cannot move from task to task and 'just do it'. For example, if you need to write a blog article, make sure that part of the time you schedule is for research and planning.

Time for reactionary

You may need to consider building some time to respond to things which happen during the day. Perhaps give some time to responding to emails, returning phone calls and so on. I am a big fan of not having emails open all the time and I rarely answer the phone. It is far more time-effective to return the call when I am ready. Do not allow someone else's sense of urgency become yours unless it is right to do so.

Commit it to paper

When we write things down, two things happen. Firstly, there is a feeling that we have released cognitive power by moving it from the mind to the paper. Secondly, by writing it down, we have 'made it real' and therefore committed to action.

Talking of which, what are you going to commit to on your action plan?

Quote

Remember what Jim Rohn said

"Either you run the day or the day runs you"

Action plan

....

....

....

....

....

....

....

....

....

....

....

....

....

Don't forget to include by when you will complete each task by.

Habit 8 - Review

What went well?

We often concentrate so much on the negatives that we forget to recognise what went well. This is a very important exercise. It is important to congratulate yourself on doing well. If it is something you are going to do again, then repeating or even increasing what went well is important too.

What could have been done even better?

By framing the question as "even better", it is predicated on whatever you did as being done well in the first place. This is a great way of asking for feedback either of yourself or others.

Carry forward - beware of procrastination

Are there certain tasks which you find yourself carrying forward into the next day repeatedly? Be honest with yourself: are you procrastinating? If so, push that task to the very top of the list for the next day and do it before anything else. You will thank yourself for it.

Got distracted?

Did you become distracted? If so, why? Focus is the exclusion of all else, so you may need to make some changes to your environment. For example, close down all those extra browser tabs; switch your phone off; work in a different location.

How do/did you feel?

Think about how you felt at different points during the day, both physically and emotionally. How do you feel now, having completed your working day?

Keep it brief!

I think keeping your review to around five minutes is all that you need. This certainly is not about writing some sort of report on your findings; it is about understanding how you can be better tomorrow.

Coordinate thinking

Ask yourself the following questions:

+/+   What am I doing that I want to do more of?
+/-   What am I doing that I want to do less of (or stop)?
-/+   What am I not doing that I want to start doing?
-/-   What am I not doing that I want to continue not doing?

The last one can seem somewhat odd. Keep it in the context you are working in. For example, if you are not going into the office, that may be something you wish to continue not doing.

Top tip

Do not spend too long reviewing or else you make get into analysis paralysis

Action plan

....

....

....

....

....

....

....

....

....

....

....

....

....

Don't forget to include by when you will complete each task by.

HABIT 9: meditation

Habit 9 - Meditation

The importance of meditating

We live in a time of information overload. Our brains are over-stimulated by communication, information, television, radio, mobile phones... and so it goes on, every waking minute of every day.

Meditation is about focusing on ourselves. It is about quietening your mind to external stimuli. It is about shutting down your inner voice and slowing down all that it going on in your mind. Focus is closing off everything other than the one thing we want to concentrate on.

When meditating, we can then become relaxed and alert simultaneously.

By occupying the conscious mind, we open up the unconscious mind.

How to meditate

Personally, I like to use an app to guide me through the meditation process and am using Calm to do that. In the simplest of ways, you can find a quiet space, sit with your legs crossed and keep saying "om" out loud for long periods of time. You can also find that certain activities may have a meditative effect. For example, I find that with glasswalking and yet I would not recommend that you do that at home! Again, find a way that you find easy. It should be an easy process and one that you enjoy.

When to meditate
I would suggest that as long as you are in a safe position to, then there is never a bad time to meditate.

I can happily meditate first thing in the morning, during the day or at the end of the day. Each will give me a different experience. One of my favourite times is before exercising. I have often found that if my mind feels full or I have a lot of self-talk going on or that I am worried about something, it tends to have a negative effect on my workout. With a clear head, I can push myself further.

It is good for your mind, body and soul.

Remember, to create a habit, it may take anywhere from 18 to 254 days, with the average being 66 days. My advice is that you make meditation part of your daily routine.

Quote

Anonymous
"The quieter you become, the more you hear"

Action plan

....

....

....

....

....

....

....

....

....

....

....

....

....

Don't forget to include by when you will complete each task by.

DAILY ROUTINE

Daily routine

It has taken me some time to really work out what I think my daily routine should be. I knew I needed one and I had a rough idea of what I thought should be included. I have played around with it and adjusted it to a point where I think I am there. That said, I will always consider it a work in progress, as I do with everything in life.

One thing I definitely learnt was that the first step should have been to have decided what I wanted to do before trying to work out the timing. It ended up that I recognised that getting up at 4.30am during the week gives me enough time to get my 'set up' routine done before starting the 'day proper'.

On the next double page, I share my personal routine. You are more than welcome to copy it, model it or perhaps just use it as inspiration to work out your own routine.

I love getting up at 4.30am. No, I honestly do! It makes me feel alive and that I have somehow won the day. You know when you get that excitement rising when you are about to go on holiday? I get a little of that.

Until very recently, I was a snoozer. I would set multiple alarms for back up and hit snooze on my main alarm. Sound familiar?

A wise man told me that how we run our life in one area is how we run it in all areas. What I have taken this to mean is that by snoozing the alarm and lazing around in bed, it is like me sending out the message that I can wait. There is little urgency.

That does not sit well with me. What kind of message does it send out to the universe? So, I decided that I needed to change it. At first, I managed to get it down to my alarm going off at 4.30am and then my second alarm going off at 4.45am signalling time to get up. I knew this was still lazy and so from then on I made a commitment to myself: when the alarm goes off, I stop the alarm and I get up. Guess what? I do not miss the extra time I used to spend in bed.

I am also going to bed earlier than I used to. It still needs to be earlier, I think, and yet it takes some adjustment to get used to. My target time is 9.30pm. All I am missing out on realistically is watching more television.

Flexibility is important. I am often away with work. I also have functions to go to or evening networking and so on. I allow myself the flexibility that I need to do the things I choose are important enough to do. Wherever possible, I stick to my morning routine though. I like it - it gets my day going in the best possible way and I feel it is of paramount importance to follow.

If you want something different, you have to do something different.

What will be different about your morning routine?

Say bye to...

jumping straight into the day

taking in the news

negative people

energy-zappers

off-plan work

limiting beliefs

procrastination

environmental stressors

checking email first thing

unresourceful behaviours

SAM
DYER

Morning routine

0430	Alarm
	Get up and dressed
0445	Why / Goals / NBG
0500	Motivate & Educate
0600	Meditate
0615	Exercise
0710 - 0830	Shower, breakfast, get kids ready for school

Sprints

50 minutes on - 10 minutes off
from 0830 if no school run
from 0930 if on school run

choice

every action or inaction is your own

#nanodecisions

WHY
reaffirm your purpose

GOALS
does the day align with the 6 week plan?

NBG
visualise the big picture

MOTIVATE
watch or read something motivational

EXERCISE
do something active

REVIEW
brief review of the day

PLAN
plan the next day ahead

MEDITATE
clear the mind and relax

Action plan

....

....

....

....

....

....

....

....

....

....

....

....

....

Don't forget to include by when you will complete each task by.

FOUNDATIONS

Foundations

Nutrition

A good healthy diet is very important. If you eat a poor diet then you are going to struggle with you energy levels and alertness.

I am not one who only eats organic. I am sure I probably have too much red meat and I also like something sweet every so often.

As many would agree: it is about balance.

Sleep

Different people need different amounts of sleep. Find what works best for you. It is important to find your own rhythm and keep to the routine. REM sleep is great for reducing stress and you need a good sleep pattern to get the right amount.

Open mind

Keep an open mind. Allow people to challenge you. Listen to those who have a different opinion to your own. Over the years, I have had my mind changed and enlightened to many things. Some of the most fundamental have been around my belief (as it is now) that we are all moving energy matter. Linked with that is that the body and mind are one system. And linked with that is quantum physics and quantum healing. All are concepts which I did not previously hold much belief in, if any. What might your mind be changed on if you are open to change it?

Growth mindset
Dr Carol Dweck wrote a fantastic book called Mindset. Her work centres around the difference between fixed mindset and growth mindset.

Fixed mindset characteristics
Believe that your intelligence is static
Avoids challenges
Get defensive and give up easily
See effort as fruitless or worse
Ignore useful negative feedback
Feel threatened by the success of others
You may never reach your full potential and may plateau early unless you make some changes.

Growth mindset characteristics
Believe intelligence can be developed
Embraces change
Persist in the face of setbacks
See effort as the path to mastery
Learn from criticism
Find lessons and inspiration in the success of others
With this mindset, you are likely to reach even higher levels of achievement.

If this is a concept that interests you, I highly recommend Dr Dweck's book.

Values

We live our lives by our values and beliefs. They are developed at an early age and then refined as we get older. By our late twenties, they are strongly in place.

Remember this from Habit 1? A value is something that we live our life by - a set of moral codes you could say. Some are contextual, ie they apply to work or home or being a parent etc. Some are core values, which remain fixed in any context. It is normally one or two words, often linguistically known as a nominalisation (to make a verb into a noun). So, you will recognise yourself, things like: happiness, health, honestly and so on.

By engaging the services of a certified NLP coach, for example, you can go through a values elicitation process to understand what your values are and the hierarchy they are arranged in. The coach can also help you resolve any conflicts present or change the hierarchy if you wish to increase or decrease the importance of a value.

Learning

I believe that we should constantly learn. This could be as simple as taking in something useful that someone tells you. It could be watching a TEDtalk or taking a course. Do whatever works for you and makes sense in the context at the time.

What are you going to do differently from today?

Action plan

....

....

....

....

....

....

....

....

....

....

....

....

....

Don't forget to include by when you will complete each task by.

Action plan

....

....

....

....

....

....

....

....

....

....

....

....

....

....

Don't forget to include by when you will complete each task by.

Action plan

....

....

....

....

....

....

....

....

....

....

....

....

....

Don't forget to include by when you will complete each task by.

Action plan

....

....

....

....

....

....

....

....

....

....

....

....

....

Don't forget to include by when you will complete each task by.

Action plan

....

....

....

....

....

....

....

....

....

....

....

....

....

Don't forget to include by when you will complete each task by.

Action plan

....

....

....

....

....

....

....

....

....

....

....

....

....

Don't forget to include by when you will complete each task by.

Enquiries

The best way for me for you to get in touch is via email to hello@samdyer.co.uk.

My websites provide a lot of information and I would encourage you to check if you can find what you are looking for there first.

coaching   samdyer.co.uk
LMP event   lifemorepowerful.com

If you are interested in engaging me for coaching or training, please free to to email, call on 020 3633 6055 or book a call in via samdyer.co.uk.

For any other enquiries, including press, please email or call in the first instance.

Further copies of this book are available directly from samdyer.co.uk.